Storyworlds

Linking Minds and Imagination through Literature

MARLENE ASSELIN

NADINE PELLAND

JON SHAPIRO

Pippin Publishing Limited

Copyright © 1991 by Pippin Publishing Limited
150 Telson Road
Markham, Ontario
L3R 1E5

Designed by John Zehethofer
Edited by Dyanne Rivers
Printed and bound by the Alger Press

Canadian Cataloguing in Publication Data

Asselin, Marlene, 1949–
    Storyworlds

(The Pippin teacher's library ; 2)
Includes bibliographical references.
ISBN 0-88751-030-2

1. Literature – Study and teaching (Elementary).
2. Language arts (Elementary). 3. Reading
(Elementary). 4. Children – Books and reading.
5. Interdisciplinary approach in education.
I. Pelland, Nadine. II. Shapiro, Jon E.
III. Title. IV. Series.

LB1575.A77 1991   372.64'044   C91-094105-X

ISBN 0-88751-030-2

10 9 8 7 6 5 4 3 2 1

CONTENTS

Introduction *5*

Stepping into Storyworlds *8*

Choosing Storyworld Books *11*

Creating Storyworld Experiences *15*

Formal and Informal Reading *15*
Teacher and Children in the Storycircle *16*
Establish an Atmosphere for Learning *17*

Exploring and Extending Storyworlds *21*

Challenges *21*
Learning Centers *23*

Storyworld Themes: A Framework for Learning *38*

The Space Theme in Action *39*
The Changes Theme in Action *54*

Bibliography *68*

Space Theme *67*
Changes Theme *68*
Professional References *71*

To our families —
Rob, Renee, Nicole, Michael, Rob, Ami,
Chana, Ezra, Toni, Kylie and Tara —
and to children everywhere
who explore the worlds created by books
and to the teachers and parents
who open these worlds to them.

. . . .

INTRODUCTION

Several years ago, *Time* magazine gloomily reported on the number of children failing their kindergarten "exit" examinations. Yes, paper and pencil examinations for five-year-olds! This is a disturbing indicator of what is happening in the field of education for young children. Or perhaps we should be referring to this phenomenon of earlier and earlier formal instruction and testing as "miseducation." Surely, some of those five-year-old children had difficulty with the fine motor control required to mark tiny areas of an answer sheet or to select the correct response from an array of similar alternatives. Surely, many of them could not have taken a formal test without first practicing test-like tasks. Are activities like these, which are likely presented in the form of worksheets, really what young children should be doing in school? We don't think so.

In earlier years, the preschool and kindergarten were seen as places where children had an opportunity to become socialized to school and group activities at the same time as they developed their awareness of important concepts through play. Developmentally appropriate experiences were thought to foster the sense of industry and competence required for children to be successful in subsequent encounters with formal instruction.

Somehow we seem to have lost touch with our knowledge of how young children learn. Both schools and parents assume that because children have had daycare or preschool experiences, they are ready for the same model of instruction as older children. In his book, *Miseducation: Preschoolers at Risk*, David

Children learn through experience and by manipulating concrete objects.

Elkind challenges this assumption, saying, "Early instruction miseducates, not because it attempts to teach, but because it attempts to teach the wrong things at the wrong time. When we ignore what the child has to learn and instead impose what we want to teach, we put infants and young children at risk for no purpose."

The methods and materials used with children aged three through six are of critical importance. Because they learn through experience and by manipulating concrete objects, educational experiences for this age group must focus on activities and projects, not subject-matter knowledge. Our experience has indicated that children's literature provides an excellent jumping-off point for developing these projects and activities. While the response-based curriculum set out in this book has been successfully implemented in preschool, kindergarten, first- and third-grade settings, the uses of children's literature and the experiences presented are valuable for any age group. After all, as Edward Ziegler said, "Every child is a magic period. We must be just as concerned for the six-year-old, the ten-year-old, and the sixteen-year-old as we are for the four-year-old."

We call our approach to children's literature the "story-world" experience because we believe that stories become worlds of fantasy for young children. And, by extending their storyworld experiences to other curriculum areas, the children have an opportunity to experience and re-experience the wonderful new worlds they have discovered in their imaginations.

The storyworld environment is rich in real literature and vibrant with color, life, print and children's representations of their growing knowledge. It is a busy place, filled with the resources children need to seek out the answers to their questions and loaded with suggestions for hands-on activities that encourage them to experiment and take risks in creating new knowledge for themselves. It is also a place for sharing, a place where the imagination is free to soar and where challenges can be taken up in a warm, supportive atmosphere.

The storyworld experience begins when teachers promote personal engagement with quality literature that encourages children to explore, imagine and play. Not all children's books, however, facilitate this and they must be selected carefully. As we invite you to begin encouraging the children in your care to create their own storyworlds, we will lay the foundation for a literature-based curriculum within a responsive environment. In doing so, we will examine critical aspects of the storyworld experience and offer suggestions for selecting appropriate literature and establishing a classroom environment that encourages personal responses and fosters exploration and risk-taking as well as for extending the experience across the curriculum. We will also share specific examples of storyworld experiences that have worked in our own classrooms. It has been our experience that storyworlds promise life-long learning for everyone — children, teachers and parents.

STEPPING

INTO STORYWORLDS

As children, many of us were read richly textured stories by our parents, grandparents, brothers and sisters. We then drew upon these experiences to create our own imaginary worlds — storyworlds — while playing in our homes. Fewer of us were provided opportunities to create storyworlds in classroom settings. In some classrooms, stories are not read to young children at all. In others, stories are used as a management tool to quiet the group. Some teachers, even those with the best intentions, "basalize" stories by using instructional methods drawn from commercial reading materials.

A key element in successfully helping children create storyworld experiences is the selection of books. Nearly everyone recalls the story of the ugly duckling, for example, but do we remember how we experienced it as children? The little duckling lived in a world of loneliness, ridicule and rejection. The sorrow that pierced his heart as a result of his fateful ugliness climaxed as he abandoned himself to the frozen waters of death. But a miracle happened. Birth followed death, just as warmth followed cold. The duckling, transformed into a swan, was revered for his beauty, and the swan came to know tranquility, admiration and friendship. Heard this way, *The Ugly Duckling* is more than a children's fairy tale. It is the story of some of the most powerful emotions of life.

Children respond to these emotions. As teachers, we have observed the importance of feelings for children. We have seen their tears and smiles as the story is being told and shared their delight in their paintings, music and role-playing as they reconstruct the storyworld themselves in various centers around the room.

The first step in creating storyworlds in your classroom is to understand the importance of emotional content in books. Stories with strong emotional content stand in sharp contrast to the fluff often passed off as children's literature. Because children find this content easy to relate to, they can re-create these feelings in many different ways.

If you examine your own tastes in literature, you can probably identify the importance of emotional content in defining your own favorite stories. After all, the emotions highlighted in literature are often those that have meaning in our own lives and, as we identify with them, we are drawn into books. How often have you said, for example, "I really got into that book!"?

While the meaning of a book resonates through its emotional content, narrative is the structure through which this is expressed. Many children are already familiar with narrative because they have listened to, for example, stories told in their own families and because adults have regularly read storybooks to them. As they mature and gain experience with the world, their awareness of narrative becomes more conscious. For most, narrative is a natural framework for structuring experiences, an important "cognitive resource" that facilitates intellectual development, expansion and refinement. To observe the interaction of narrative structure and emotional content, let's look at what happens when a story is read.

The teacher is sharing *Swan Sky*, a recently written Japanese fairy tale. This time we are not in a warm farmyard as in *The Ugly Duckling*, but far, far away on a cold northern lake. At just the right moment, all the swans but one lift off and begin to fly from north to south, from winter to summer. The family of the one who stayed also remains behind, trying to coax her to join the others. As the children hear this, they begin to make connections to another story they have heard — the cold, a swan who is singled out, her inability to join others. A thought occurs: will she, too, change into something else like the ugly duckling? The children listen now on two levels for they have connected with the story emotionally and, intellectually, they are anticipating the outcome.

The story continues: "That night they rest together in the moonlight. The young swan buries her head in her feathers. As she sleeps, her family gathers around her. Before morning, she dies."

Death is announced clearly and directly. But there is still birth — not for the one but, this time, for the whole flock of swans when they safely reach their nesting grounds in the warmth of spring.

As they experience the similarities in the structure of these two stories as well as the power of the emotional content, the children reach a new understanding: the cycle of life occurs on many scales. They can then take this new knowledge and re-express, re-create and re-experience it at other centers throughout the room.

Children learn a great deal about literacy from the story-world experience. If they are read to frequently, they develop a sense of story. This includes acquiring important understandings about books, about print and about story form. The acquisition of these understandings is a consistent predictor of success in beginning reading.

At the most basic level, children learn that print carries meaning and the learned anticipation that there will be a meaningful story is one of the foundations for developing reading comprehension. At this level, children learn that it is primarily the letters and words on the page, not the illustrations, that carry the story. They also expand their awareness of how books work — that they must be held right side up, that one proceeds from left page to right, and that the print is processed in this direction as well. It is especially important to take time to develop some of these very basic concepts with children whose first language is not English and those whose homes are not rich in literacy experiences.

Listening to stories also familiarizes children with literary conventions that alert readers to such things as the beginning of a story and the statement and resolution of the problem. An awareness of these conventions helps develop reading comprehension.

In addition to fostering the ability to read for information, the paramount goal of the literacy curriculum is to develop an enjoyment of reading. While literature-based programs promote positive attitudes toward reading, many traditional forms of literacy instruction actually work against this goal.

Positive experiences with good literature support the development of favorable attitudes toward reading, contributing to the motivation to become a reader and to continue to be a reader for a lifetime.

Choosing Storyworld Books

Because the quality of the literature read to children is so important to the storyworld experience, careful consideration must be given selecting titles for core books (single books for reading aloud to children), support books (those that relate to a literary theme) and curriculum books (those that represent and reinforce areas of study in the classroom).

Examples of all three types of books are found in the bibliography. You may wish to assess whether these titles fit the criteria established by the questions that follow. As you become familiar and comfortable with the relationship between the questions and the books listed in the bibliography, you may wish to begin asking the same questions about books you are considering for use in your own classroom.

Even if you feel uncertain about your ability to recognize a "good" book, don't be timid. Become a library-lover, explore the children's section and check out — and read — lots of books. Initially, it might help to look for award-winners or to browse through reviews of children's books in professional journals, magazines and newspapers. The very best indicator, however, is the response of the children in your classroom. Look to see if the themes introduced by the books are carried into the their play, whether on their own or with friends.

While core books are the foundation of the storyworld experience, support and curriculum titles are extensions of selecting the single book. Once you begin to develop a feel for what makes a good core book, the ability to decide on literary groupings and theme collections will follow quite easily. Support and curriculum books enable connections to be made either on a small scale, such as books that display similar literary patterns, or on a broader scale, such as books that relate to an area of study.

Does the book connect with children's lives?

When choosing storyworld books, be aware that plot is not necessarily the most important consideration. As in *The Ugly Duckling*, content that appeals to the emotions tends to interest children and encourage further exploration. This is readily seen in the total interest displayed during storytime and in the children's play when they make comments such as, "You be the bad guy and I'll be the good guy," "Say we're like Ninja Turtles and we'll catch all the bad guys," or "I'll be the prisoner in the dungeon and you come and set me free." Stories that pit good against evil or despair against hope are usually good choices for creating storyworlds.

Is the content important to children?

The questions that are important to children are virtually universal and remain remarkably consistent from generation to generation. Children ask some difficult questions. Where did people come from? How did the sun and the moon get into the sky? What does flying like a bird feel like? Books that deal with the questions children ask always generate successful storyworld experiences.

Does the book engage children's imaginations?

Successful storyworld experiences are based on children's extensions of the literature they are read. The heart of a response-based curriculum is the imagination of the child. Television has the effect of dulling the imagination because it always shows the viewer everything. Good imaginative literature, on the other hand, builds and encourages the uniquely human ability to create fantasies in the mind. Myths, fairy tales and legends are the best sources for imaginative storyworlds. Careful consideration should also be given to the illustrations in a book, for these should form a visual story that enhances the text and stimulates the imaginary processes.

Is the content organized as a satisfying narrative?

Earlier, we mentioned the importance of narrative in structuring play experiences. Storyworld books have a clear setting, a cause-and-effect chain of events, emotionally vivid characters and a satisfying resolution.

Are the emotional themes and underlying questions related?

These themes and questions may be related on the basis of their similarities — or their differences. For example, the theme of the tormented stepsister (Cinderella) who is rewarded for her purity with earthly love and wealth occurs in well over 100 versions. As well, practically every culture has stories that address such basic questions as how did the world begin? How did the sun and moon get into the sky? Why are there seasons? By exploring these stories, children can begin to compare how different peoples have dealt with these questions over time.

How do these literary patterns connect?

Literary elements other than theme include setting, plot, character, language style and genre. Subtle plot connections, such as those between *The Ugly Duckling* and *Swan Sky* contribute to children's ability to make meaning by allowing them to relate knowledge and feelings generated by one story to another. On the other hand, differences in literary elements promote the development of different expectations from stories. Children will, for example, come to expect different things from a story set in ancient Greece than from a story set in urban North America. Familiar language patterns, such as refrains, also contribute to comprehension. With experience, children learn to recognize even the most subtle similarities and differences among literary forms.

Are individual differences accommodated?

Books that support a literary theme should also be selected to accommodate the wide range of developmental and individual backgrounds, needs, interests and abilities that exist among the children in many classrooms. Some children, for example, are fascinated by certain language patterns while others may be attracted to a particular style of illustration. North American children come from a variety of ethnic backgrounds and should have the opportunity to investigate stories with familiar settings as well those set in different cultures or periods.

Does the collection include both fiction (contemporary and traditional) and non-fiction?

Once the children are hooked into storyworlds, it is natural and appropriate that they have access to a range of reading materials that is as broad as their responses. Now is the time to share the many forms of literature — poetry, chants, concept books, realistic fiction, information books — as well as to provide continuing exposure to traditional folktales, fairy tales and myths. It is never too early to introduce children to the informational styles of writing commonly found in the content-oriented textbooks they will encounter during their later elementary school years.

Is there the potential for a wide range of extensions to the children's learning?

Storyworld experiences can be extended into esthetic, historical and scientific knowledge. Curriculum collections include books about the arts, about people and places, about the natural world and about the human-made world. In this way, literature can become an extension of or even the foundation for the curriculum.

Are individual and developmental differences accommodated?

The reading level of the text is not necessarily an important consideration at this point. Children can derive valid learning experiences from well-illustrated "adult" reference books as well as from early reader books. Remember, too, that in a group of children, there are bound to be a range of interests. Anticipate as best you can, then add books to the collection as you observe these interests developing.

. . . .

CREATING

STORYWORLD EXPERIENCES

Effective early childhood programs are well-rounded, for they recognize that all aspects of the child are equally important to self-development. Social, emotional, esthetic and physical development must be considered alongside language and intellectual development. Learning is facilitated when children are able to bring their own experience and knowledge to tasks. Thus, the storyworld environment is child-centered, inviting exploration, interaction and the formulation of personal responses. The teacher serves as a catalyst for learning by interacting with children and designing centers and activities that meet their needs.

Formal and Informal Reading

There are many ways to share stories with children. While the large-group storycircle is familiar to everyone, stories can be read in small, informal group settings as well. Parents, volunteers and visiting siblings welcome chances to share this particular experience with children, for they often find small groups less intimidating and more manageable.

With a little advance planning, a rewarding visitor-volunteer storyreading program can be developed. Providing "guest" readers with an opportunity to observe how you read to children is an effective way of ensuring that the experiences will be positive for everyone.

Stories can also be shared in other ways — through puppets, felt boards and creative drama, for example. Be sensitive to the preferences of the volunteers and visitors, as some may not be entirely comfortable with this method of sharing.

A variety of props should be readily available so that the children themselves can retell a special story that was shared in the storycircle. These props should not be restricted to the storycircle area, but should be integrated into other centers in the room. For example, space-journey supplies might be located at the imagination center, Orpheus's harp might be found at the music center and Vulcan's forging tools at the block center.

THE CLASSROOM AS A DYNAMIC LIBRARY

Not only should props be available around the room, but also books should be within easy reach everywhere. Storyworlds should be as close to children's fingertips as they are to their hearts. We started by scattering a few support books around the room and it was not long before the library "corner" expanded to become the library "classroom." It made sense! Instead of training the children to restrict their emotions and imaginations to the library corner, we opened the whole classroom to literature.

Teacher and Children in the Storycircle

In a literature-based classroom, the teacher plays an important role in introducing children to stories and preparing the storyworld environment. Stories engage both the heart and the mind. Because individual reactions to stories may be quite similar or very different, *all* the responses of *all* the children must be valued.

One of the first hurdles children face in school is the development of trust. The quality of the teacher's interactions with the children will influence their willingness to trust in themselves, their peers and the teacher.

In one classroom, a teacher was observed reading *Jack and the Beanstalk* to her class. She asked a typical question, "What sort of boy was Jack?" One child eagerly waved his hand and, when recognized, loudly stated, "Jack was a bad boy." The teacher, clearly puzzled, responded, "What? Why on earth do you think that?" A little more timidly, the boy mumbled, "'Cause Jack stole and then . . . and then he *killed* the giant."

16

Rather than accepting this thoughtful, albeit unusual, interpretation, the teacher declared, "No, that's not right. Everyone knows that Jack is the hero." The student, his eyes now cast down, didn't participate for the remainder of the storytime. In fact, over the next few weeks, he tended to mumble a defeated "I dunno" in response to the teacher's questions. Rather than affirming his willingness to take a risk and valuing his response, the teacher had dismissed it as "incorrect." In the process, his trust was shattered.

In the storyworld experience, the feeling generated by storytime is one of closeness, warmth and safety. Opening up and sharing these responses require conditions that foster intimacy and involvement. As children come to trust that the teacher will value their reactions to stories, they will respond openly and more often. In this way, storytime becomes the place where unformed responses can be gently shaped and learning can begin.

Establish an Atmosphere for Learning

The classroom should be a safe and stimulating community of learners where responses can be shared, listened to and explored by individual children, teachers and the class. Establishing this kind of atmosphere is vitally important when designing a response-based curriculum that encourages children's responses, both intellectual and emotional, and promotes interaction with the materials. Much of the success of this approach depends on the teacher's understanding of his or her role as facilitator. Arriving at this understanding often involves examining assumptions about teaching, learning and knowledge.

As adults, it is easy for us to assume that our knowledge of the world is somehow better than children's. Those who adhere to this view tend to use a mimetic or "banking" approach in the classroom, believing it is the teacher's job to fill the empty vault — children's minds — with something they believe is of worth.

Others take a different approach, recognizing that while, as adults, we may certainly have amassed more experience, this experience makes our knowledge different from, but not necessarily better than, children's. For those who hold this transformative or midwife view, teaching involves not telling but enabling, supporting and guiding learning. In other words, the role of the teacher is to assist in giving birth to new knowledge.

What kinds of teacher behaviors encourage children to do such things as ask questions, risk demonstrating their knowledge to those who might know more, and challenge themselves to weave the thread of stories into their own worlds? Interactive teaching is not a free-for-all, but rather a tightly and subtly orchestrated performance whose timbres, shapes and melodies pulse in response to the players and the moment.

Teachers can achieve this lofty-sounding goal by incorporating specific interrelated practices into the story: by encouraging esthetic engagement, inviting dialogue and fostering higher level thinking.

ENCOURAGING ESTHETIC ENGAGEMENT

Perhaps the simplest and most effective practice is the one most frequently disregarded. We are often in such a hurry to instill the "right" knowledge in children that we neglect one important aspect of learning, namely reflection. This takes time . . . and silence.

Thus, our first suggestion is to tell or read the stories straight through without giving in to the temptation to interrupt the flow in order to "teach" something. Remember that the guided reading activities and practices that accompany basal reading programs are not intended for use with children's literature.

Many children are subjected to a lot of verbal distraction during storyreading in their homes. These children, in particular, will probably need regular and extended opportunities to simply listen to and enjoy stories before they are ready to articulate their responses.

As we listen to stories, we use our imaginations to conjure mental pictures, or images, of the setting, characters and events. Some children, however, may not have had much practice at this kind of image-making. Teachers can encourage this by inviting the children to close their eyes during storyreading and make a picture in their heads of where the story takes place, what the characters look like or how one event follows another. Guide them to visualize one specific aspect of the story. Suggest that they share these visions with a partner or invite them to compare them with other experiences involving similar settings, characters or themes. For example, share Van Gogh's painting, "Starry Night," when reading a story set at night; play Gustav Holst's musical composition, *The Planets*, in connection with mythological stories, or take them to a cultural dance and drama event when reading literature involving a different culture.

INVITING DIALOGUE

Teachers can encourage children to articulate their thoughts and feelings about stories by initiating a dialogue themselves or by responding to comments made by the youngsters. The responsive teacher is at once sensitive and analytical, quick to seize opportunities to explore and extend the children's understanding.

Successful techniques for initiating dialogue include:

— inviting questions and comments. "Looking at the cover of this book, what do you think this story might be about?"
— providing information. "This story is so old that people knew it before there was writing. Stories like this were passed down from generation to generation by word of mouth."
— encouraging predicting and risk-taking. "Listen for the clues that will tell you what is going to happen before you hear the whole story."
— modeling thinking. "I *thought* Professor Noah would end up in a better land than the one he left because that's what happened in the first Noah story. But I'm surprised he traveled backward in time instead of forward to a better time — that's usually what happens in space stories."
— linking a story theme to children's experiences. "Lee's family comes from the same country as this story."

Teachers should also be sure to:

— show spontaneous appreciation for stories. "I like it when I read a story from my grandma's country. It helps me understand her better."

— allow time for the children to respond.
— value the children's responses. This means following up your acknowledgment of a child's response by affirming what he or she has shared rather than imposing your own assessment of its value. "You heard a clue that helped you predict what would happen to the wolf."
— "scaffold" responses by zeroing in on opportunities to increase interactions with the book or peer group. "Laura told us yesterday that Anansi had to go through three tests to get the golden box of stories and, today, George noticed that Little Badger had to do the same to get fire for his people. Then some of you said there might be something special about this. We should keep our ears open to stories that have tests and see if authors usually have the character do them in sets of three."
— provide opportunities for children to extend their interaction with the story, primarily by suggesting challenges, a technique explored in the next chapter.

FOSTERING HIGHER LEVEL THINKING

Because teachers set the stage for the responses they expect from children, they must provide opportunities that foster thinking on a variety of levels. Making personal connections to characters, recalling another version of a story or stating factual information about a setting represent one kind of response. Explaining how the sequence of events in one story is similar to that of another, providing evidence that stories are related or debating the difference between a nature myth and a scientific theory are other kinds of responses.

Teachers can guide the children's critical responses to literature by encouraging them to ask questions, make and confirm predictions, draw inferences and connect ideas. These interactions should invite specific, rather than global, responses. When teachers guide children to use clear and specific language, they are enabling the development of knowledge — of self, of others and of the world.

If one of your goals is to help children develop their capacity for critical thinking, you will find a literature-based curriculum an ideal vehicle for achieving this. Because literature communicates with children at the most basic levels, the motivation for critical thinking is strong.

. . . .

EXPLORING AND EXTENDING

STORYWORLDS

To finish reading a story is not to end the story-world experience. In fact, formal storyreading is only the first step into this rich, imaginary world. To encourage children to continue the journey, we must provide them with the time, place and materials necessary to re-experience and explore the themes and textures of the stories told. This can be achieved by presenting challenges and organizing opportunities for free exploration at learning centers scattered throughout the room. While stories are the foundation on which children's learning is based, activity or learning centers provide the means by which they can construct, explore and extend their knowledge.

Challenges

Because children do not necessarily articulate all that they know, teachers need to facilitate experiences that go beyond listening to and retelling stories. Children need time to linger over and revise their initial responses to what has been read to them. Activities such as art, writing, music, movement, drama and construction provide opportunities for personal meaning-making and social representation of the stories. As they engage in these activities, children have access to many forms of language as resources for learning.

While these activities may be guided by the teacher, they are fundamentally child-centered. In other words, the teacher may plan experiences and provide materials, but the children decide the direction and length of the interaction. Typically, these experiences occur at activity or learning centers, special areas designated for and stocked with materials that will encourage specific activities. However, not all classrooms have enough space to accommodate a full range of centers, nor must experiences be limited to centers. An effective way of guiding, rather than directing, children is by presenting challenges. These are open-ended questions and activity suggestions written on large strips of paper and displayed like signs around the room. A challenge may be as straightforward as "Find something to share about space from your book" or as subtle as "Paint the colors of loneliness." Challenges can be taken up by individuals or shared with partners or groups. Here are some examples:

ART

Sketch a lunar landscape.
Paint your feelings about flying.
Design a flag for a new space colony.

MOVEMENT AND DRAMA

Make a kitchen for a space house.
Make a happy nest for the ugly duckling.

MUSIC

Compare a morning song and an evening song.
Tell a story with the talking drums.

CONSTRUCTION

Build a maze so the minotaur cannot escape.
Find a way to keep the animals on Noah's ark dry.
Supply our space station for a one-year journey.

MATH AND SCIENCE

Design a mosaic pattern for a temple.
Sort the kinds of wood in Paul Bunyan's lumberyard.
Plant a terrarium and watch your own forest grow.
Dissect fish to see how they survived the flood.

Learning Centers

There are many advantages to using learning centers as an organizational structure in your classroom. First, centers provide a rich and varied learning environment that accommodates a variety of learning styles and fosters the social, emotional, artistic, physical and intellectual development of individuals in an integrated, meaningful setting. As children respond to the stories they hear, connections between what is already known and what has just been experienced will be made in ways that are personally meaningful to each individual. Therefore, when possible, many different learning centers should be available so that children will have opportunities to create and respond to storyworlds in their own ways.

Because the structure of learning centers is flexible, the curriculum can be introduced through free exploration of materials before formal instruction is given. Once learned, skills can be reinforced and new concepts can be applied in a meaningful context. In this way, learning is extended and enriched.

A centers approach can also help children move towards some of the general goals of education. Self-reliance and self-confidence, for example, are fostered as children are encouraged, first, to make their own choices and, second, to become as independent as possible. Learning centers that provide open-ended, meaningful and relevant first-hand learning experiences are best for developing youngsters' confidence. Centers stocked with developmentally appropriate activities and materials engage children in higher level thought processes. As well, process-oriented activities foster the development of self-confident, independent learners. Possessing the confidence to know you can achieve is a powerful motivating force. This inner awareness can become the catalyst that sparks life-long learning, as the reward for success comes from within, not from a need to please the teacher or parent.

Open-ended, developmentally appropriate play and learning activities at centers also foster the construction of knowledge in personally relevant and meaningful ways. Children learn through play and through social interaction with their peers and adults. Centers provide children with opportunities to work and play independently and cooperatively within a meaningful context, to follow their own interests, to make decisions and assume responsibility, and to discover and learn at their own rates and in their own styles through first-hand experience.

When using this approach, guidelines must be clearly outlined so that children know what is expected of them in terms of behavior, care of materials and equipment, clean-up, consideration of the rights of others, and their individual responsibilities as learners (for older children, this might involve discussing and setting out the quality and quantity of work produced).

The teacher's role is to create a safe and rich learning environment, to facilitate and guide learning by interacting with individuals and working with small groups on skills, and to create a continuing cycle of assessment and evaluation through observation, the collection of authentic data and keeping records of what each child can do. Based on the data collected, the teacher decides on the next step needed to help the learner move forward. Then the assessment cycle begins again.

In summary, learning centers provide the vehicle for responding to stories. They allow children to create and re-create storyworlds through role-playing, dramatizing and representing what they feel, imagine, think and wish to find out. They provide a means of constructing knowledge through the use of imagination, social interactions, language and thinking processes. They provide experiences that enhance social, emotional, language and intellectual development. The descriptions of learning centers that follow provide some ideas for creating a rich learning environment that will ensure success for all children.

BLOCK CENTER

Blocks provide almost unlimited opportunities for learning through play and for integrating many curriculum content areas. Mathematical concepts involving patterning, classification, size, shape, space, measurement (volume, area, length, height, width, depth), number, order, fractions and symmetry are experienced and learned incidentally during block play. Scientific processes such as observation, experimentation, discovery, trial-and-error, formulating hypotheses and arriving at conclusions also take place while children play with blocks. At the same time, concepts relating to balance, stability, gravity, weight, inclined planes, ramps and the interaction of various forces as well as the properties of matter begin to form. Design concepts relating to form, pattern, symmetry and balance are also developed. Eye-hand coordination, visual perception and large and small muscle control are part of the physical development facilitated by block play.

The development of thought and language through social interactions is an integral part of block play. In addition, as children engage in the very complex process of stepping back from and transforming the "self" into a symbolic new person, they are growing in their understanding of symbolic representation, an underlying awareness necessary for grasping concepts involving numerals and literacy. Reading and writing activities are also generated at the block center as children label, name, plan, map and communicate their ideas or realms of fantasy.

Block play fosters social and emotional development as feelings of accomplishment and self-confidence are nurtured through the shared construction of children's visions. Initiative, responsibility, cooperation and respect for the work and rights of others are developed as well.

The possibilities for representing ideas in curricular areas like social studies are also extensive and include such concepts as cognition of symbolic representations, concrete three-dimensional mapping and the social, cultural and physical structures of communities. Through play, children develop a sense of self emotionally, socially and physically as they experiment, explore and imagine themselves in various roles.

The power of the imagination as expressed through socio-dramatic play is an important component of play at the block center. Structures or objects are created and, through imagination, transformed into representations of the children's ideas, fantasies and explorations of themselves and the world around them.

Equipment

At least one set of solid wooden blocks including a variety of geometric shapes such as cones, triangles and cylinders.

One set of hollow blocks.
One set each of plastic animals, people, cars and trucks.
One train set including wooden tracks.
A road-sign set (these can be made at the art center).

WATER TABLE CENTER

Like the block center, the water center also provides unlimited possibilities for integrating learning into play. One of the most obvious is the emotional satisfaction children derive from playing with water. Many a parent has placed a young child in the bath because of its calming effect. The same strategy can be applied at the water table center to soothe a child who is feeling upset.

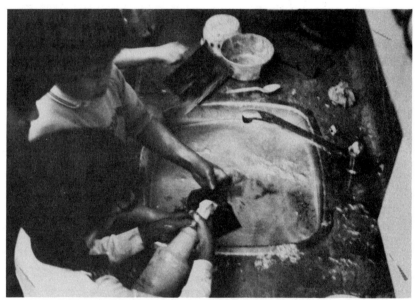

Social interactions foster the development of thought and language.

Social interactions are fostered as children communicate their feelings, ideas and sense of joy. Growing out of these social interactions at the water table is the development of thought and language, the vehicle for expressing thought.

Key content areas enhanced at the water center are science and math, often in an integrated fashion. For example, concepts relating to liquid measurement are acquired at the same time as the properties of liquids are explored. Through the exploration, investigation and observation generated during play, theories and hypotheses are tested and retested, analyzed and synthesized.

The free-form, unstructured nature of water as a medium for play makes it very engaging for children of all ages. With the addition of materials such as food coloring, soap and egg beaters for making bubbles, the possibilities for using the water center are limited only by the imagination.

Equipment

Collections of containers, beakers and bottles of all shapes and sizes (if parents are asked to donate these, be sure they did not previously contain dangerous substances).
Collections of measuring spoons and cups.
Plastic tubing, pumps, a water wheel.
Food coloring and liquid soap for bubble-making.

SANDBOX CENTER

Sand is another material that, by its very nature, generates unlimited possibilities for engaging the imagination. Like the block and water centers, the sandbox center lends itself to the integration of curricular areas such as math and science. As well, thinking strategies relating to spatial awareness and relationships are fostered. These might involve the planning and organizing of spaces into a community or natural environment such as a moonscape, three-dimensional mapping, the symbolic representation of one object by another, or any other activity the child chooses to engage in to make meaning of the environment or real and imaginary experiences. It's worth noting that it is often difficult for young children to separate what is real from what is imagined. Their perceptions of the world are often quite different from those of adults!

Equipment

A sandbox big enough for at least four children to stand around.
Sterilized sand.
A set of scoops, shovels and measuring containers.
Theme-related props.
A plastic sheet or tarpaulin for the floor under the sandbox.

It is at this center that some of the most profound thought and learning take place as children think their way through their accumulated life experiences and, through dramatic play, find expression for ideas that have been incubating. As they pretend that an object is something else or transform themselves into other personas in order to explore concepts such as what it would be like to be an astronaut, they are engaging in the very complex cognitive act of symbolic representation. When they make this imaginary transformation, they are learning about symbolism by internalizing, in personally meaningful ways, a very abstract cognitive process. Experiences with symbolic representation are the foundation upon which an understanding of the symbol systems of letters and numbers is built.

Children must have many opportunities to participate in dramatic play so they can begin to comprehend this abstract process, then build the system for themselves within their own minds. Children will often create their own symbol systems until they recognize a need for a standardized system in order to communicate with others. Concepts of literacy and numerals that begin in storyworlds and the realms of the imagination are acted out at the dramatic play center. Using the imagination can be a first step in the process of learning to read and write.

Equipment

Theme-related props.
Dress-up clothes.
Interesting pieces of cloth for draping into costumes and capes.
Dishes, cutlery, pots and pans (these can be toy items or donated by parents if made of plastic).
Tables, chairs and toy or real items such as basins, ironing boards, etc.

WRITING CENTER

This center provides opportunities for children to represent their ideas and to express themselves, in written form, at their own level of development. This level might be the scribbling phase, the pictorial representation of ideas, the emergent level of symbolization and spelling, or the fully developed stage characterized by correct grammar and spelling.

Materials provided at this center should be portable so that writing activities can extend throughout the classroom to meet the needs of children who wish to write as part of their play at other centers. For example, they may want to write "messages" or grocery lists at a playhouse created at the dramatic play center, map or label construction projects at the block center, or record information or a discovery while conducting a science experiment.

For older children or those who are ready to move beyond emergent writing and towards standard forms of literacy, the "writing process" should be introduced. This involves generating ideas, writing a draft, editing, proofreading and publication. It should be noted that it is unnecessary to move through the sequence in a lock-step progression each time a child writes. Children love to create their own "published" books, but may not be developmentally ready or have the desire to work their way through the complete process.

If journal-writing is a free-choice activity at the writing center, it can foster emergent writing, emergent spelling and reading. Writing will promote reading which, in turn, stimulates thought processes and more writing. It's worth noting that there is no place for stenciled skill-and-drill, fill-in-the-blank worksheets or workbooks in a child-centered, process-oriented learning environment. Activities like this turn children off learning because they are usually boring bits of busywork that do not promote higher level thought processes.

Equipment

Pencils, felt pens and markers.
Unlined paper in assorted sizes, shapes and colors (some lined paper may be included at centers for older children).
Scissors, glue, glue sticks, rulers, a hole punch, staplers, staple removers.
Typewriter.
Stamps.
Booklets to write in.

Not only are computers communication and problem-solving tools that will assume even greater importance as we move into the 21st century, but children also enjoy using them. When children become accustomed to using computers at a young age, many later problems involving computer "illiteracy" may be avoided. Computers can also provide an alternative to the writing center. If a modem is also purchased, it will enable children to communicate with other classes in other areas, a powerful motivator for writing! Keep in mind, however, that software must be selected carefully as some programs are little more than electronic worksheets.

Equipment

A computer with a simple word-processing program, a drawing program and, if possible, a voice synthesizer (the latter, while not critical, can be useful for programs for non-readers).
A color monitor.
A printer.
Floppy disks, one for each child, stored in a disk container.
An assortment of age-appropriate programs.

Because books are integral to a rich learning environment, this center is a focal point for and provides a springboard to a child-centered curriculum and should be designed with flexibility in mind. Books should not be restricted only to the library center, but should be accessible to children throughout the room. Children need to be encouraged to use books at any time as a resource to augment their learning in any curriculum area and in any part of the classroom. Thus, math concept books would be found in the math center, special theme-related books would form part of a science display or experiment center, and books would be available in the art center.

"Big books" that have been used in group shared reading experiences should be available at the library center where children can return to them for informal personal or shared "buddy" reading with a peer or older student. Young children enjoy the repetition and patterns often found in big books.

Equipment

Literary groupings of books.
Theme collections of fiction and non-fiction.

FLANNEL BOARD CENTER

A component of the library center, the flannel board center provides children with an opportunity to retell stories and, in so doing, make the story their own. This activity encourages them to create their own imaginary extensions and personal interpretations of the stories while promoting an understanding of story form as they move through the narrative from beginning to end. In addition, they also come to understand literary conventions and develop a sense of literary language. Children need opportunities to tell stories in many different ways before they ever begin to write them down.

Equipment

Felt board, felt characters and props labeled and stored in sealed plastic bags.

PUPPET THEATER CENTER

Another component of the library center, the puppet theater center can also engage young imaginations in powerfully stimulating ways. Like the dramatic play center, this center invites children to explore the persona of a character. For example, through playing with a puppet, a shy child might be able to explore the role of a powerful, outgoing character. Often children will use puppets as a means of working through real-life problems. With puppets, they can dramatize a scenario and, if the conclusion doesn't satisfy them, they can explore a different one.

Puppets also provide opportunities for language exploration and development. Children carry on internal dialogues or communicate verbally as they interact with the puppets and develop stories, activities that activate, develop and extend thought processes.

Equipment

Cardboard theater (wood can be dangerous).
Assorted puppets, commercial or handmade.

A third component of the library center, the flip chart center is a place where children can enjoy rereading poems, songs, rhymes and re-experiencing stories that were previously shared as a group. A flip chart displaying these shared charts should be readily available for them to reread on their own or with friends in an informal "buddy" reading session in which two or three children support and help each other.

Equipment

Flip chart with a wooden backing (metal frames are fine for displays but difficult for children to write on).
A collection of teacher-created charts and pocket charts with story strips.
Paper and felt markers.

MATH CENTER

Piaget demonstrated that children learn abstract concepts best when they manipulate real, concrete objects. For example, if they have two marbles plus one more marble, they can concretely conceptualize the equation, $2+1=3$. As they manipulate the marbles, all their senses are involved in the process of building knowledge. Because they can see and feel them, they do not have to imagine two, one or three in the abstract.

As they work with concrete objects, children begin to conceptualize our adult symbol system as well as complex processes such as multiplication or division. Teachers can help guide children towards learning these processes by posing open-ended challenges such as, "Make up a number story." The resulting stories may range from a simple collection of five objects to a complex depiction of the process of division. All stories must be accepted as valid in relation to the level of knowledge the individual has attained.

Free exploration of a variety of manipulative objects is what young minds need in order to build a firm foundation of understanding before formal instruction is attempted. Knowledge about numerals must be pieced together by the individual child. Individuals construct their own understanding and knowledge of numerals through their own personal experience and learning style. Recognizing patterns, classifying, ordering, measuring and understanding sequence

Children learn abstract concepts by manipulating concrete objects.

and equivalence are all necessary experiences in building the foundation for working with the symbols, systems and abstract codes of math.

Once a foundation has been established, more structure and direction can be introduced to children who are ready by posing meaningful challenges that require the practical application of concepts learned. The materials provided at this center should be adjusted according to the theme under study.

Equipment

A wide variety of manipulative materials such as plastic interlocking blocks, number trays, pegboards, geoboards, attribute and table blocks and Cuisenaire rods.
An abacus.
Sets of objects for counting, sorting, ordering and classifying, such as buttons, bread tags, etc. (these should be stored in small boxes).
Paper and pencils.

SCIENCE (EXPLORATION) CENTER

If children are to be prepared for the 21st century, not only will they need to be risk-takers, but they will also have to be flexible, fluid, creative and critical thinkers. The scientific process closely parallels the thinking process. Observation, experimentation, hypothesis formation, testing and the drawing of conclusions are critical to both. Thus, scientific inquiry within the classroom fosters the development of thinking strategies that will provide some of the skills necessary for success in the future. As well, children can experience the joy of discovery and the pleasure of learning about such things as nature, natural phenomena, physical properties of matter, chemical reactions and the reaction of forces. Not only do they role play the scientist — they are a scientist! These experiences can be powerful motivators for learning and become the catalyst for developing life-long interests.

Children can contribute to and help develop the science center by bringing objects of interest from home or suggesting activities or experiments for others to try, processes that nurture feelings of self-worth and responsibility. In addition, writing and reading skills can be enhanced and practiced as children use books to research the answers to their questions, record their findings to report at sharing time or prepare a written personal response to what has been learned. This response might be in the form of their own "published" book, a poster or perhaps an experiment report. The possibilities for integration with math are obvious because of the calculations using numbers to measure, compute and record data.

Equipment

A wide variety of theme-related, real-life objects and equipment to aid children in investigating, experimenting with and testing ideas and theories (eg., scales, magnifying lens, microscopes, tweezers, etc.).
Teacher-initiated displays and demonstrations such as a terrarium, aquarium, crystal garden, plants, etc.

COOKING CENTER

Because the process of cooking, of course, causes changes in both the physical and chemical properties of the food, the cooking center is closely associated with science. Math concepts are also integrated into the work of this center as children must measure and compute ingredients for their culinary creations.

Equipment

Recipes written on charts (use rebus forms for non-readers).
Cooking utensils as required by the recipes.
Electric frying pan, wok, assorted pots and pans.

LISTENING CENTER

The listening center provides enjoyment for those who wish to listen to music without disturbing others. It can be used for listening to stories or for telling personal stories, strategies that help support beginning readers individually or in small groups. In addition, other audio-visual equipment, such as filmstrip projectors, can be used to add variety and extend experiences at this center. Listening posts can also be incorporated into the library center with clear guidelines for use so that others will not be disturbed.

Equipment

Headphones, cassette player, phonograph.
Filmstrip projector.
Theme-related tapes and filmstrips.
Age-appropriate records and tapes.

INTEREST CENTER

Very special things such as art objects, a collection of natural items, a costume from another culture, a musical instrument, etc. might be found at this center. These might be brought in by the children, parents or the teacher. Items should be sturdy, able to stand up to handling by children. Depending on the activities and theme being studied, this center can be combined with others such as the science centre.

In addition to opportunities for esthetic and cultural appreciation, this center provides plenty of scope for extending learning into other areas of the curriculum. Because children are invited to contribute, they take pride in their role in building the learning environment. Respect for the possessions of others is also fostered.

Equipment

Collections of theme-related objects such as maps, special paintings, etc.

The music area can be the center of much joy (and much noise!) as children express their creativity and let their imaginations soar through rhythm, song, dance, movement, playing instruments and using musical language such as poetry, chants, limericks or song lyrics.

Music can be a very powerful teaching aide for it integrates the senses and the emotions. Learning to read can be fun when the words are sung! Facts can be learned by adding rhythm or singing them. Because this center can be noisy, guidelines for use will need to be discussed and posted.

Equipment

Good quality rhythm and percussion instruments.
Notation paper for "composing."

ART CENTER

Self-expression, exploration, creativity and personal responses are encouraged at the art center. Pre-cut paper shapes complete with instructions for putting them together do not foster artistic development. In process-oriented classrooms, children are not asked to color stenciled pictures neatly and correctly. Rather, their need to explore line, shape, texture, depth, color and design using a variety of media is recognized and accommodated. For young children, the process is often more satisfying than the product. When the process has been completed to a child's satisfaction, the product will sometimes be discarded without a thought.

When children think through their own projects, making decisions based on their own analysis of what is needed in terms of color, shape and design, thinking and learning are happening. Young children do not need to be told how to do art, they *feel* it. Through art, they learn independence and gain personal satisfaction and confidence in their own abilities.

As with some other centers, firm guidelines must be set out for using the art center. In addition, thought must be given to its location. It's a good idea, for example, to place it on tiles rather than a rug and to take measures to protect the surrounding environment and the children's clothes. This center should also be close to the construction center so that materials can be interchanged.

Equipment

At least two easels and one table.

A variety of colors and types of paint such as water colors, tempera, and finger paints.

Paper in various sizes, textures and shapes, including finger-painting paper.

A variety of paintbrushes, rollers and sponges.

Materials for printmaking and screen frames.

Potter's clay kept in a covered plastic container.

Plasticine and boards, as well as plastic modeling clay in various colors with utensils for cutting and rolling shapes.

CONSTRUCTION (PROJECT OR IMAGINATION) CENTER

At this center, children are encouraged to express their imaginations in three-dimensional form by building their own "creations." In the process, they create any number of representations of their knowledge of the world around them. These might become props for their storytelling, puppetry or dramatic play. As children visualize, plan and revise their plans while constructing their projects, they learn various thinking strategies. Practical mathematical applications, for example, are integrated into the process. Construction center activities are suitable for individual and cooperatively planned projects, fostering the growth of self-confidence as children experience success in a real-life activity.

Advance planning and guidelines for behavior at this center are essential because of the potential for noise and, more important, problems with safety issues.

Equipment

A woodworking table with child-size tools and a vise.

Soft woods in various lengths and shapes.

Nails, screws, wood glue and sandpaper.

Colored cellophane, tissue and glittery paper in various sizes.

Small boxes of assorted shapes and sizes.

Plastic bottles and containers, aluminum plates, cloth scraps, netting, thread and needles, paper cups, plates and bags.

Paper rolls, bits and pieces of cardboard, string, wool scraps.

Scissors, glue, stapler, hole punch.

Collections of natural objects such as twigs, stones, shells, sand, chicken bones, moss, etc.

. . . .

STORYWORLD THEMES:

A FRAMEWORK FOR LEARNING

A thematic approach, in which classroom activities are integrated with and linked to a particular theme, facilitates learning by connecting concepts within a framework that promotes understanding. Topics are not taught in isolation. Children build knowledge as they make sense of a variety of experiences through active involvement in activities at the learning centers.

We have selected two themes — Space and Changes — to illustrate the kinds of activities that can be generated at learning centers when this approach is used. Within each are mini-themes designed to encourage further exploration and re-creation of the storyworlds introduced through the initial storybook experiences.

The lesson suggestions set out on the following pages are intended to be exactly that — suggestions. While challenges are presented in a sequence that facilitates concept development, flexibility should be the watchword as the children's interest guides the direction of activities. The activities suggested can be extended to other centers as well.

In reflecting on teaching, Kahlil Gibran wrote that the teacher "does not bid you enter the house of his wisdom, but rather leads you to the threshold of your own mind."

A response-based curriculum built on a foundation of exceptional literature provides children with a stimulating environment for continued intellectual growth. How fortunate we are, as teachers, to be able to observe, facilitate and enjoy that growth!

The Space Theme in Action

PROJECTED FLOW OF CONCEPT DEVELOPMENT

Sky Stories
The Olympians
Multicultural Myths and Legends

The Planets

The Universal Desire to Fly
Icarus
Leonardo da Vinci

Flying Machines
First Flight

Remember, the children's needs, interests and abilities should be your guide when setting the direction for this theme. Be alert to and ready to accept their suggestions for further activities and mini-themes that will help extend their story-world experiences. Space flight, environmental issues and mythical heroes are just a few of the related areas that might be explored.

. . . .
Book: *The Olympians* by Leonard Everett Fisher
. . . .

To introduce the Sky Stories mini-theme, try placing the "feature" title, *The Olympians*, as well as other books containing Greek myths and legends on a table or the carpet. Invite the children to look through them by saying something like, "Find out about the Olympians."

As they respond to what they see, the children will naturally break up into discussion groups. Collaboratively, they will help each other "read" using a variety of methods including picture clues. Observing the children as they make meaning in this way makes it very clear indeed that "a picture is worth a thousand words."

After the children have had plenty of time to explore the books informally, set the stage for extending their learning by inviting them to share and discuss what they have found out. Thus, new possibilities for learning are opened up.

The teacher or a child who reads might then read aloud one or two of the stories about the Olympian gods. Discussion will undoubtedly become enthusiastic and interest will be high as the children enter their own storyworlds on the wings of Hermes, the thunderbolt of Zeus, or the chariots of Hades.

Challenges at Centers

Art

Visualize yourself as one of the Olympians and make a body tracing of your character. Write about your character.

Construction

Make the symbol for your sky character. Build Mount Olympus or the temples of the gods.

Science

Find out about air.
Find out about the sky.

Music

Make music for the gods.

Write a song to one of the gods.

Cooking

Make ambrosia.
Make a feast for the Olympians.

Dramatic Play

Become an Olympian.
Make a costume.

Sandbox

Construct Mount Olympus.

Follow-Up Book

Space Songs by Myra Cohen Livingstone

· ·
Title: *A Story, a Story* by Gail Haley
· ·

This Anansi legend tells about the sky god who keeps all the stories of the world in a golden box. Anansi, the spider man who is the village storyteller, weaves a web up into the sky country to ask the king to share the story treasures with the people on Earth.

This story provides a wonderful springboard to process writing. Emergent writing will proliferate as the children make up their own stories. If parents are invited to a feast to celebrate, the children might tell their stories and share African foods.

Challenges at Centers

Writing or Computer

Write a story that can be placed in the "golden" story box for everyone to enjoy.

Construction

Make a class "golden" box to store story folders for school and to use at home. Use cardboard, gold paint and glitter.
Make puppets of the story characters.

Science

Investigate and study spiders and their webs. Keep a spider alive in the classroom for a few days. What does it eat? How does it make a web? Keep a spider journal. Be sure to set it free when you are finished.

Block

Build the sky king's kingdom or the spiderman's village.

Art

Make the three things that the spiderman had to capture before he got the story box.

Cooking

Cook an African feast using yams, peanut butter and chicken.

Music

Make some African music for your celebration at the feast.

Puppet or Flannel Board

Make a puppet show or flannel board presentation of the story.

Follow-Up Book

Anansi the Spider by Gerald McDermott

. . . .
Book: *Why the Sun and the Moon Live in the Sky* by Elphin-
ston Dayrell
. . . .

Throughout time, people from all cultures have wondered
and asked questions about the heavenly bodies. Children, too,
are fascinated by the solar system.

One of the most powerful motivators for learning is the
need to seek answers to our own questions. This ancient
legend provides a wonderful springboard to extending growing knowledge. Responses to this story may require several
days as children prepare props or costumes and develop their
own ideas. Another class — or the principal — might be
invited to view their creations.

Challenges at Centers

Construction

Make a stick puppet of one of the water people, the sun
or the moon using a stick, tissue and cellophane.

Science

Find out about water. Experiment with it. Make notes
about what you discovered to share with others.

Library

Find out about the sun and moon. Make a booklet about
one of them.
Find out about a creature that lives in the water.

Writing

After you have found out about a creature that lives in
the water, tell all about it in a booklet.

Water Table

Find out how much water will fit into various containers.

Follow-Up Book

The Seventh Night of July by Paula Franklin

Book: *Arrow to the Sun: A Pueblo Indian Tale* by Gerald Mc-Dermott

The illustrations in this book are as powerfully engaging as the story and should provide an important focus for the children's responses.

The challenges that must be overcome by the central character should also be examined as they offer valuable lessons about story form and sequence. These will be learned incidentally through the children's involvement in the activities at the centers where ideas can be represented in a variety of ways.

Challenges at Centers

Art

Sponge paint a picture of part of the story like Gerald McDermott did in the book. Then arrange it in sequence with pictures created by other children.
Make a paper mosaic of the sun.
Make a Pueblo clay pot.

Construction

Weave a Pueblo blanket
Make a Pueblo house or village. How will you make stairs to get up and down?

Science

Plant some maize (corn) and record how it grows.
Experiment with some of the plants to see what they need in order to grow healthily.

Cooking

Cook some corn-on-the-cob to eat for snack.
Bake corn bread to eat with butter.

Dramatic Play

Make the story with your friends. Which character will you be? What will you use for props?

Theme: Space   Mini-Theme: The Planets
· ·
Book: *National Geographic Picture Atlas of Our Universe* by
Roy A. Gallant
· ·

This book links the mythological gods of Mount Olympus to
the planets of our universe in very powerful, graphic ways.

If this book, and others about the planets, are placed on a
table or group area carpet, the following challenge might be
presented on the "greeting" chalkboard as the children enter
the classroom: Find out about our universe. Tell a friend about
what you have found and tell the class at sharing time. Use a
book mark if you need to.

As the children discover that the names of the planets are,
in many cases, the same as those of the gods — Mars, Jupiter,
Neptune, Venus, Pluto, Mercury — the ensuing discussion
will become the basis for an introductory lesson on the planets
of our solar system.

This book depicts the gods and their symbols along with the
planets, reinforcing the idea that symbols are a way of convey-
ing meaning. Depending on the children's interest, the learning center activities may span a period lasting from several
days to a few weeks.

Challenges at Centers

Library

> Find out about our universe. Tell a friend what you dis-
> covered.
> Find out about one planet.

Art

> After finding out about our solar system or a planet,
> fingerpaint a planet and add it to the solar system
> mural. What colors does it need? Where does it belong
> in the solar system?
> Draw the solar system.
> Spatter-paint a galaxy and sprinkle sparkles on it.
> Paint the colors of the universe.
> Make a mural of the universe with some friends using
> string-, sponge-, and spatter-painting in combination.

Construction

> With some friends, use paints and tissue paper scraps to make the sun.
> Build a model of our solar system.
> Make a model of a planet using papier mache and a balloon.

Sandbox

> Make a moonscape.

Dramatic Play

> Be an astronaut going on a journey into space. What will you need? How will you go?

Writing or Computer

> Send messages from the command center to astronauts on a spacecraft.

. . . .

Featured Artist: Vincent Van Gogh

. . . .

Books are not the only source of inspiration for challenges and it is important to provide opportunities for children to respond to art forms other than literature.

Works by great artists can generate the same kinds of esthetic and emotional responses as literature. Van Gogh's painting, "Starry Night," is a perfect example. It depicts his representation of his feelings about, his esthetic response to and his knowledge of the sky. Children should be encouraged to respond to this painting, as Van Gogh did to the night sky, in their own way. Their works can be displayed beside the feature artist to demonstrate that their creations are equally valued.

Challenges at Centers

Art

Make a "Starry Night" painting.
Express your feelings about the sky or the night like Vincent Van Gogh.
What does the universe look like to you? Paint it.

Library

Vincent Van Gogh is a very famous artist. Find out about his life.

Writing

Tell Vincent Van Gogh's story.

Theme: Space   Mini-Theme: The Universal Desire to Fly

Book: *Sunflight* by Gerald McDermott

The simple text and strong visual images of this book tell the story of Icarus in a powerful way by exploring the universal themes of desire, longing and weakness and by depicting the conflicts between light and darkness and the power of the imagination and the suppression of ideas.

Through this book, young children can begin to make personal meaning of the human condition on deep intellectual and emotional levels. Their responses to and extensions of their experience with the story will demonstrate its powerful impact. This phase of the mini-theme may last several days.

Challenges at Centers

Block

Build the king's castle.
Build a maze for the castle dungeon.

Construction

Make the wings that Icarus and his father built.
Make a maze game.

Art

Pretend you are one of the characters and make a body tracing of yourself. Join with other characters to make the Icarus story on a wall mural.
Paint the color of Daedalus's sorrow.

Science

Find out how far Icarus had to fly to touch the sun.
Find out about the sun. What is it made of? Why does it shine and why has it continued to shine so long?
Explain the sun's light to a friend using a flashlight and a ball.

Writing

Write instructions explaining how to fly.
Write a story about darkness and light, good and evil, or joy and sorrow.

Book Title: *Leonardo da Vinci* by Alice and Martin Provensen

You might introduce this three-dimensional pop-up book by sharing one of the pages and saying, "People have probably watched birds and wanted to fly since the days of the cave people. They have had many ideas about how they too could fly. Here is one person's idea. Here is another . . . . This man was an inventor." Children will undoubtedly remark that da Vinci's ideas resemble modern-day helicopters and gliders.

Challenges at Centers

Construction

Use your imagination like Leonardo and invent a machine.
Make something that flies.
Make a plan for a flying machine and then follow your plan to build it.

Science

Find out about air.
Make a paper airplane and fly it.
Study the night sky like Leonardo.
Find out why birds don't fall out of the sky.
Find out about the stars.
Make a star map.

Art

Leonardo was a painter. Express your ideas with paint like Leonardo.
Leonardo was a sculptor. Make a statue with clay.

Library

Find out about the life of Leonardo da Vinci.
Find out about other inventors.

· ·
Book: *Professor Noah's Spaceship* by Brian Wildsmith
· ·

Professor Noah takes the animals on a journey into space, looking for a pristine planet where they can escape the destruction of their forest habitat and the pollution on Earth.

This story is likely to spark discussions about a variety of complex issues dealing with the environment, endangered species, pollution, destruction of forests and acid rain. In the process, many opportunities will arise for using complex thinking strategies such as hypothesizing, analyzing, synthesizing, generalizing and evaluating.

Developing real-life solutions that the children can implement themselves may be a very exciting outgrowth of this mini-theme and may, in fact, provide a springboard to a full-fledged theme devoted to the environment.

Challenges at Centers

Writing

Write a personal commitment pledge to show your concern for our planet.
Make a map to another planet or galaxy.

Art

Fingerpaint the polluted Earth and a cleaned-up Earth.
Make clay animals and a spaceship.

Construction

Build Professor Noah's spaceship.

Science

Find out what plants and animals need to live. Be a scientist and make up an experiment demonstrating what you found out.

Dramatic Play

Make up a play about the story. What would the animals say to each other?

Library

Find out about distant worlds. Is there one we could go to? Why?

Follow-Up Group Activity

Try a teacher-led, guided visualization of the story with sound effects created by rhythm instruments . . . take off into other worlds and perhaps return — in a different time or theme!

· ·
Book: *The Glorious Flight* by Alice and Martin Provensen
· ·

In this book, the intense human drive to fly is explored in the context of a family story. Through the story, children can experience the many trials, failures and new attempts involved in producing a flying machine. They will come to understand that airplanes weren't invented in a single day, but resulted from developments over time as ideas were built one upon another. They may even realize that in the future they may contribute to the development of new technology.

Challenges at Centers

Science

Using balloons and straws, find out about air.
Make clouds. What are they?

Art

Paint the colors of the sky. Paint the clouds.
Paint or draw flight pictures. Paint a "glorious" flight.

Construction

Make a time-line showing the historical development of flight using drawings and dates.
Make a map showing the view from an airplane.

Writing

Pretend you are an early pilot and write a journal of a first flight.

Dramatic Play

Get ready for a glorious flight.

Math

Calculate the distance between two places you want to fly to. If you fly at X miles (km) an hour, how long will the flight take? How much fuel will you need?

Follow-up Book

Regards to the Man in the Moon by Ezra Jack Keats

The Changes Theme in Action

PROJECTED FLOW OF CONCEPT DEVELOPMENT

Cycles of Change
Life Cycle of Plants
Human Life Cycle

Transformation
Choices

Families over Time

Remember, the children's needs, interests and abilities should be your guide when setting the direction for this theme. Be alert to and ready to accept their suggestions for further activities and mini-themes that will extend their storyworld experiences. Our changing world, the evolution of animals and machines, changes in the states of matter and changes in thinking, feelings and perspectives are just a few of the related areas that might be explored.

Theme: Changes   Mini-Theme: Cycles of Change

Book: *From Seed to Pear* by Ali Mitgutsch

The life cycle of humans and the growth of families over time are only two interesting examples of change. *From Seed to Pear* can help explore the cycles of change. This exploration may develop in many different directions, leading to further mini-themes that can include topics dealing with the life cycles of plants, animals and insects.

Challenges at Centers

Writing

Make a seed book. Tell a seed story.

Construction

Plant various types of seeds. What will they need to grow?

Art

Paint a seed story. Use seeds to make patterns or mosaics.

Math

Count and sort seeds into egg cartons. Organize them by size.

Science

Set up experiments to find out what seeds need to grow. Label the experiments. Make graphs and keep records of what happens.

Follow-Up Book

From Grain to Bread by Ali Mitgutsch

. . . .
Book: *The Garden of Abdul Gasazi* by Chris Van Allsburg
. . . .

Imagination and the transformation of a character are the important aspects of this story set in a garden of changes. Throughout the ages, children's minds have been captivated by that very unique human characteristic — the imagination.

Challenges at Centers

Art

Paint a garden picture

Sandbox

Design a garden.

Science

Plant flower seeds. What do they need to grow? Keep a journal about your seeds — what they are and how much they grow every few days.

Construction

Make a map showing where the boy went in the story. Show where he began, where he went next and where he was at the end.

Follow-Up Group Activity

Plant an outdoor garden.
Go on a neighborhood walk to look at gardens.

Follow-Up Book

A Rose in My Garden by Arnold Lobel

Book: *A Child is Born: The Drama of Life before Birth* by Lennart Nilsson

Children are fascinated by the beginnings of life, curious about how they came into the world. Books like this help answer some of the most powerful questions of their young lives, building bridges to understanding the changes taking place around them. Their interest often progresses from interest in themselves to interest in their families and their histories, a process that can spark a mini-theme on family roots.

Challenges at Centers

Group Activity

Invite children to bring in, with their parents' permission, baby pictures and place these on a large piece of colored paper that everyone can sit around. Challenge them to identify classmates and draw their attention to details with questions like, "Which do you think is the youngest baby? The oldest? Which can walk, talk, etc.?"

Dramatic Play

Play house and role-play families working together and taking care of babies. How do you feed a baby?

Writing

Make a book called, "When I Was a Baby."
Make a time-line of firsts in your life.

Water Table

How do you bathe a baby safely?

Art

Represent yourself as a baby, as a toddler.
Make a life-sized cutout called "Me."

Cooking

Make baby food.

Follow-Up Book

Where Do Babies Come from? by Margaret Sheffeld

Book: *Love You Forever* by Robert Munsch

This particular Robert Munsch book deviates from the expectations many children may have of his stories. Rather than presenting a humorous treatment of typical family situations, the author explores the transitions that happen during a lifetime in a very sensitive manner. Many children may be able to identify personally with this material. Teachers should be aware that the transitions depicted in the book can be a powerful experience for the children.

Challenges at Centers

Construction

> Make an integrated poster of yourself in the past, present and future by mounting a baby picture, drawing a picture of yourself as you are now and writing a story about what you will be like as an adult.

Writing

> Write a letter to your parents to tell them how much you appreciate the things they do for you and what you can do for them.
> Send a card to someone you love.

Music

> Write a love song.

Art

> Paint the colors of love.
> Paint a love story.
> Paint or draw a picture of someone you love.

Interest

> Find pictures that show people who love each other.

Group Meeting Area

> Discuss the various kinds of love: love between mother and father, children, family, pets, etc.

. . . .

Book: *The Ugly Duckling* by Hans Christian Andersen

. . . .

Literature can engage children in abstract higher level thinking processes and transformation stories are particularly good vehicles for promoting these processes and providing a sequence for connecting ideas. Books like *The Crane Wife, The Crane Maiden, Dawn, The Wild Swans* and *Bird Song,* as well as *The Ugly Duckling* are all stories about transformations.

The Ugly Duckling is a classic story that has captivated generations of readers because it reaches their emotions as it explores deep feelings such as rejection, loneliness, love and insecurity. In addition, the story indirectly explores opposing themes of cold and warmth, darkness and light, rejection and acceptance.

Children identify strongly with these feelings and eagerly express their own in a variety of ways as they respond to the challenges at the centers. This tale also helps develop children's sense of story — setting, problem, climax and resolution.

Challenges at Centers

Art

> Fingerpaint background murals for the setting of the story — the farmyard and house, the frozen pond and the beautiful lake. You might cut fingerpainted paper into strips to make the reeds.

Writing

> On paper folded into three sections, retell the story.

Dramatic Play

> Dramatize the story. How did the duckling feel?

Construction

> In a group, use brown paper bags, glue and paper feathers to make cutouts of the characters to place on the background murals.
> Make stick puppets for a puppet play of the story.

Sandbox

Make the farmyard.

Science

Investigate the cycle of the duckling's life as he changes from egg to chick to "duckling." See the book *Egg to Chick*.

Follow-Up Book

Go Tell Aunt Rodie by Eliki

Follow-Up Group Activity

After reading *Go Tell Aunt Rodie*, sing the song together.

Theme: Changes   Mini-Theme: Transformation
....
Book: *Dawn* by Molly Bang
....

This transformation story is interchangeable with *The Crane Wife*. Though set in different cultures at different times with different characters, the themes of the two books are the same. Both invite readers to enter a gripping and compelling storyworld. The artistic details of this book also stimulate the children's esthetic sensibilities.

Challenges at Centers

Art

> Paint your ideas about this story.
> On a large wooden frame, weave with rags.

Construction

> Make the Canada goose. You may wish to use white paper for the body, stuff it with newspapers and staple. Brown construction paper can be used for the head and wings.
> Build your own boat. Sail it at the water table center.

Music

> Make music to show how the father felt, how Dawn felt, and how the little girl felt.

Follow-Up Book

> *Winter Wife* by Ann Elliot Crompton

· ·
Book: *The Crane Wife* by Sumiko Yagawa
· ·

This Japanese folktale moves the reader to think about the decisions one faces in life, the choices one must make, and the consequences of these choices. This story and those that follow can inspire children to engage in levels of thinking that many educators have considered beyond their young years.

Nevertheless, children respond emotionally and the expression of these feelings should be encouraged. Keep in mind that this expression may not be verbal. Rather, it will manifest itself in a variety of ways through a variety of media as the children work through the challenges at the centers. Later, when invited to share their creations in a group setting, the children will often be able to articulate these feelings.

Challenges at Centers

Library

Find out about cranes.

Writing

Write a journal showing what the crane wife was thinking as she wove every day.

Write a letter to the husband telling him what you think.

Construction

Build a house for the wife and husband.

Build a weaving loom.

Art

On the loom you built at the construction center, weave fabric like the crane.

Paint the colors of love and sorrow.

Make a mural of the transformations in the story.

Follow-Up Books

The Crane Maiden by Miyoko Matsutani or *The Selkie Girl* by Susan Cooper

Theme: Changes   Mini-Theme: Transformation
. . . .
Book: *Paul Klee: Art for Children* by Ernest Raboff
. . . .

Artists may represent familiar objects and ideas in surprising ways. Klee's work can spark children's imaginations as they compare the titles of the works to the paintings themselves and reflect on the transformations the artist made.

Focus on Paintings

Artists represent their ideas in many different ways.
What do you think Paul Klee's ideas were in this painting?
How did Paul Klee express these ideas? What materials does he use?

Challenges at Centers

Art

Make print shapes like Paul Klee.
Represent the way you have changed since you were a baby in a way that you think Paul Klee might have.

Writing

Tell about your painting.
Write what you think Klee was thinking about when he painted.

Construction

Measure "Klee-like" shapes, then cut them out and make a mobile or a collage.

Book: *Ancestor Hunting* by Lorraine Henriod

Children's families make an excellent resource for challenges. While you may wish to draw on this book for inspiration, focusing on the children's individual families can inspire them to create their own family stories. By delving further into their family histories and exploring their roots, they will develop a historical and geographical perspective on who they are and where they have come from. This understanding helps foster emotional and social security.

When encouraging children to engage in these activities like this, teachers must be sensitive to and respectful of changing family relationships and differences among the families of children in the class.

Challenges at Centers

Construction

Use paper to make your family house and draw or paint a family member in each window or door that opens.
Invite your family to participate in making a family tree.
Create a family crest with a coat of arms.

Library

Find out about the country of your family's origin.

Writing

Write about your family and its members. Staple your story into the "House Booklet."
Interview your grandparents and other family members and then write their history.
Write a journal about your family's trip to this country.

Art

Make clay figures representing the members of your family.

Block

Build your family neighborhood.

Cooking

Make a favorite family recipe. Put the recipe in the class cookbook.

Pretend that you are an early settler. Plan and cook a meal you might have eaten.

Interest

With your parents' permission, bring a cherished family item to school and display it. Tell about it during sharing time.

Book: *Chagall: The Master Works* by Michel Makarius

Marc Chagall tells his family story through his artistic interpretations. His paintings reflect a colorful imagination and sense of humor that captivate children. Their natural responses to his paintings can promote thinking processes through the use of higher level questioning. Examples of possible questions are provided in the lesson. The suggested activities also stress the importance of the imagination as a motivational force in the thinking process.

Focus on Paintings

> How does the painting make you feel? How does it do this?
> How do you think Chagall felt when he painted this picture?
> What do you think he was trying to say? Is there a story in this painting?
> Why do people look like they are flying? What do you think Chagall was thinking about or feeling?

Challenges at Centers

Art

> Express your imagination like Marc Chagall.

Writing

> Tell the story that you see in a painting by Marc Chagall. Give your painting a title.

Follow-Up Book

> *Chagall for Children* by Helene Lamarch

BIBLIOGRAPHY

Space Theme

Baylor, B. *Moon Song*. New York: Scribner, 1982.

Belting, N. *The Sun Is a Golden Earring*. New York: Holt, Rhinehart & Winston, 1974.

Bernstein, M. & Kobrin, J. *First Morning: An African Myth*. New York: Scribner, 1976.

Cameron, A. *How Raven Freed the Moon*. Madeira Park, Canada: Harbour, 1986.

Caselli, G. *Gods, Men and Monsters from the Greek Myths*. Text by M. Gibson. London: Lowe, 1977.

Chek, C.H. *The Sun King*. Toronto: Dominie Press, 1976.

Conner, C. & Farmer, P. *Daedalus and Icarus*. London: Collins, 1971.

D'Aulaire, I. & d'Aulaire, E.P. *Book of Greek Myths*. Garden City, USA: Doubleday, 1962.

Dayrell, E. *Why the Sun and the Moon Live in the Sky*. Boston: Houghton Mifflin, 1968.

Dickenson, T. *Exploring the Sky by Day*. Camden East, Canada: Camden House, 1988.

Fisher, L.E. *Theseus and the Minotaur*. New York: Holiday House, 1988.

Franklin, P. *The Seventh Night of July*. Agincourt, Canada: Silver Burdett, 1985.

Frazier, K. *Solar System*. Chicago: Time Life Books, 1985.

Fuchs, E. *Journey to the Moon*. New York: Delacorte Press, 1970.

Gallant, R.A. *National Geographic Picture Atlas of Our Universe*. Washington: National Geographic Society, 1986.

Garett, J. *The Queen Who Stole the Sky*. New York: Scholastic, 1986.

Gerson, M.J. *Why the Sun Is Far Away*. New York: Harcourt Brace Jovanovich, 1974.

Goble, P. *Star Boy*. New York: Bradbury Press, 1983.

Haley, G. *A Story, a Story*. New York: Aladdin, 1988.

Hansen, R. & Bell, R.A. *My First Book of Space*. New York: Simon & Schuster, 1985.

Ivins, A. *The Beginning Knowledge Book of Stars and Constellations*. New York: Rutledge, 1960.

Keats, E.J. *Regards to the Man in the Moon*. New York: Four Winds Press, 1981.

Krystyna, T. *Pegasus*. New York: Franklin Watts, 1970.

Lee, J.A. *Legend of the Milky Way*. New York: Holt, Rhinehart & Winston, 1982.

Livingstone, M.C. *Space Songs*. New York: Holiday House, 1988.

Livingstone, M.C. *The Olympians*. New York: Holiday House, 1984.

Maurer, R. *The NOVA Space Explorer's Guide*. New York: Clarkson Potter, 1985.

McDermott, G. *Sunflight*. New York: Four Winds Press, 1980.

McDermott, G. *Arrow to the Sun: A Pueblo Indian Tale*. New York: Viking, 1974. (Also available on film.)

McDermott, G. *Anansi the Spider*. New York: Holt, Rhinehart & Winston, 1972. (Also available on film.)

McLeish, K. *The Shining Stars: Greek Legends of the Zodiac*. New York: Cambridge University Press, 1981.

Proddow, P. *Demeter and Persephone*. New York: Doubleday, 1972.

Provensen, A. & Provensen, M. *The Glorious Flight*. New York: Penguin, 1983.

Provensen, A. & Provensen, M. *Leonardo da Vinci*. New York: Viking, 1984.

Rockwell, A. *The Dancing Stars*. New York: Crowell, 1971.

Simon, S. *Jupiter*. New York: Morrow, 1985.

Simon, S. *The Moon*. New York: Four Winds Press, 1984.

Sleater, W. *The Angry Moon*. Boston: Little Brown, 1970.

Wildsmith, B. *Professor Noah's Spaceship*. New York: Oxford University Press, 1980.

Wolkstein, D. *White Wave*. New York: Crowell, 1979.

Yolen, J. *The Boy Who Had Wings*. Toronto: Fitzhenry & Whiteside, 1974.

Zavre, S. *They Followed the Star*. Scroll Press, 1969.

Changes Theme

Allen, P. *Who Sank the Boat?* New York: Coward McCann, 1983.

Andersen, H.C. *The Ugly Duckling*. Retold by G. Muller. London: Octopus Books, 1985.

Anno, M. *In Shadowland*. New York: Orchard Books, 1988.

Anno, M. & Anno, M. *Anno's Magical ABC*. New York: Philomel, 1981.

Bang, M. *The Paper Crane*. New York: Greenwillow, 1985.

Bang, M. *Dawn*. New York: Morrow, 1983.

Bayler, B. *If You Are a Hunter of Fossils*. New York: Scribner, 1980.

Belting, N. *Whirlwind Is a Ghost Dancing*. New York: Dutton, 1974.

Berger, B. *Grandfather Twilight*. New York: Philomel, 1986.

Blades, A. *A Salmon for Simon*. Vancouver: Douglas & McIntyre, 1986. (Also available on film.)

Bowden, J.C. *Why the Tides Ebb and Flow*. Boston: Houghton Mifflin, 1979.

Brighton, C. *Five Secrets in a Box*. Markham, Canada: Owen Morgan Books, 1987.

Brown, M. *Shadow*. New York: Scribner, 1982. (Also available on film.)

Cleaver, E. *Petrouchka*. Toronto: Macmillan, 1980.

Cleaver, E. *How Summer Came to Canada*. Toronto: Oxford University Press, 1969. (Also available on film.)

Clement, C. *The Painter and the Wild Swans*. New York: Dial Press, 1986.

Collins, M. *The Willow Maiden*. Toronto: Groundwood Books, 1985.

Cooper, S. *The Selkie Girl*. New York: McElderry Books, 1986.

Crompton, A. *The Winter Wife*. Toronto: Little Brown, 1975.

Ehrlich, A. *The Wild Swans*. New York: Dial Press, 1981.

Eliki. *Go tell Aunt Rodie*. New York: Macmillan, 1974.

French, F. *The Blue Bird*. New York: Henry Z. Walck, 1972.

Gerstein, M. *The Mountains of Tibet*. New York: Harper & Row, 1987.

Henriod, L. *Ancestor Hunting*. New York: Messner, 1979.

Heyer, M. *The Weaving of a Dream*. New York: Penguin, 1986.

Hutchins, P. *Changes, Changes*. New York: Macmillan, 1971. (Also available on film.)

Isadora, R. *The Nutcracker*. New York: Macmillan, 1986.

Keeping, C. *Joseph's Yard*. London: Oxford University Press, 1969.

Lamarch, H. *Chagall for Children*. Judith Terry Museum Publications, 1988.

Leaf, M. *Eyes of the Dragon*. New York: Lothrop, Lee & Shepard, 1987.

Louie, A.L. *Yeh Shen: A Cinderella Story from China*. New York: Philomel, 1982.

Luenn, N. *The Dragon Kite*. New York: Harcourt Brace Jovanovich, 1982.

Lobel, A. *A Rose in My Garden*. New York: Greenwillow Books, 1984.

Luzzato, P.C. *Long Ago When the Earth Was Flat*. New York: Collins, 1980.

MacDonald, S. *Alphabatics*. New York: Bradbury Press, 1986.

Makarius, M. *Chagall: The Master Works*. London: Bracken Books, 1988.

Martin, B. *Knots on a Counting Rope*. New York: Holt, Rinehart & Winston, 1982.

Matsutani, M. *The Crane Maiden*. New York: Parents Magazine Press, 1968.

Mayer, M. *Beauty and the Beast*. New York: Morrow, 1971.

McDermott, G. *Daughter of Earth*. New York: Delacorte Press, 1984.

McDermott, G. *The Voyage of Osiris*. New York: Windmill Books, 1977.

McDermott, G. *The Stone Cutter*. New York: Viking, 1975.

McDermott, G. *The Magic Tree*. New York: Penguin, 1973.

Meyer, M. *Beauty and the Beast*. London: Collier MacMillan, 1987.

Mitgutsch, A. *From Seed to Pear*. Minneapolis: Carol Rhoda Books, 1981.

Mitgutsch, A. *From Grain to Bread*. Minneapolis, Carol Rhoda Books, 1981.

Morgan, A. *Nicole's Boat: A Good Night Story*. Toronto: Annick Press, 1986.

Munsch, R. *Love You Forever*. Scarborough, Canada: Firefly, 1986.

Murdock, P. *Deep Thinker and the Stars*. Toronto: Three Tree Press, 1987.

Newman, B. *The Nutcracker*. Woodbury, USA: Barron's, 1985.

Oakley, G. *Magical Changes*. London: Macmillan, 1988.

Nilsson, L. *A Child Is Born: The Drama of Life before Birth*. New York: Delacorte Press-Seymour Lawrence, 1990.

Provensen, A. & Provensen, M. *Leonardo da Vinci*. New York: Viking, 1984.

Puricelli, E.C. *In My Garden*. London: Neugebaur Press, 1981.

Raboff, E. *Paul Klee: Art for Children*. New York: Harper & Row, 1988.

San Souci, R.D. *The Enchanted Tapestry*. Vancouver: Douglas & McIntyre, 1987.

Schreiber-Wicke, E. *Cat's Carnival Ball*. Markham, Canada: Owen Morgan Books, 1985.

Scott, J. & Scott, L. *Hieroglyphics for Fun*. New York: Van Nostrand Reinhold, 1974.

Selsan, M.E. *Egg to Chick*. New York: J. Harp, 1970.

Sendak, M. *The Nutcracker*. New York: Crown, 1984.

Shaw, C.G. *It Looked Like Spilt Milk*. New York: Harper & Row, 1947.

Sheffeld, M. *Where Do Babies Come from?* New York: Knopf, 1978.

Shulevitz, U. *Dawn*. New York: Farrar Strauss & Giroux, 1978. (Also available on film.)

Smith, P. *Jenny's Baby Brother*. New York: Viking, 1981.

Stobbs, W. *The Little Red Hen*. Toronto: Oxford University Press, 1985.

Tejima. *Swan Sky*. New York: Philomel, 1987.

Thompson, B. *The Story of Prince Rama*. New York: Viking Penguin, 1980.

Turkle, B. *Do Not Open*. New York: Dutton, 1981.

Van Allsburg, C. *The Garden of Abdul Gasazi*. Boston: Houghton Mifflin, 1979.

Wegan, R. *Sky Dragon*. New York: Greenwillow, 1982.

Williams, K. *Masquerade*. London: Cape, 1979.

Yagawa, S. *The Crane Wife*. New York: Morrow, 1981.

Zola, M. *Only the Best*. London: MacRae, 1981.

Professional References

Bowen, E. "Can Kids Flunk Kindergarten?" In *Time*. Vol. 132, no. 5 (August 1988).

Chukovsky, K. *From Two to Five*. Berkley: University of California Press, 1963.

Cochran-Smith, M. *The Making of a Reader*. Norwood, USA: Ablex, 1964.

Dyson, A.H. "The Imaginary Worlds of Children: A Multimedia Presentation." In *Language Arts*. Vol. 63, no. 8 (December 1986).

Elkind. D. *Miseducation: Preschoolers at Risk.* New York: Knopf, 1988.

Erikson, E. *Childhood and Society.* 2nd Edition. New York: Norton, 1963.

Harste, J., Woodward, V. & Burke, C. *Language Stories and Literacy Lessons.* Portsmouth, USA: Heinemann, 1984.

Jensen, M. "Story Awareness: A Critical Skill for Early Reading." In *Young Children.* Vol. 41, no. 1 (January 1985).

Keifer, B. "The Responses of Children in a Combination First and Second Grade Classroom to Picture Books in a Variety of Artistic Styles." In *Journal of Research and Development in Education.* Vol. 16, no. 3 (Spring 1983).

Paley, V. *Wally's Stories.* Cambridge, USA: Harvard University Press, 1981.

Rosen, H. *Stories and Meanings.* Urbana, USA: National Association for the Teaching of English, 1983.

Roser, N.L. "Relinking Literature and Literacy." In *Language Arts.* Vol. 64, no. 1 (January 1987).

Shapiro, J. and White, W. "Reading Attitudes and Perceptions in Traditional and Nontraditional Reading Programs." In *Reading Research and Instruction.* Vol. 30 (1990).

Sloan, G. *The Child as Critic: Teaching Literature in the Elementary and Middle Schools.* New York: Teachers' College Press, 1984.

Wells, G. *The Meaning Makers.* Portsmouth, USA: Heinemann, 1983.

Ziegler, E. "Formal Schooling for Four-Year-Olds? No." In *A Better Start: New Choices for Early Learning.* Edited by F.M. Hechinger. New York: Walker Books, 1986.